SU &ANALYSIS

OF

BAD BLOOD

Secrets and Lies in a
Silicon Valley Startup

A GUIDE TO THE BOOK
BY JOHN CARREYROU

BY *ZIP*READS

TABLE OF CONTENTS

SYNOPSIS

The book opens on November 17, 2006, painting a picture of biotech startup Theranos, led by twenty-two-year-old Elizabeth Holmes. The board is full of seasoned professionals. The blood sample analysis technology is promising. Investors are excited. The company is valued at $165 million just three years after its founding. There's just one small problem: the technology doesn't always work. And Holmes has been faking the results in investor presentations.

When Henry Mosley, the Chief Financial Officer at the time, raised his concerns with the falsified results, he was promptly fired. This would be far from the last time such a firing occurred. Theranos, in fact, would go on for another decade deceiving investors and operating with a level of secrecy usually reserved for the Pentagon.

Elizabeth Holmes was made out to be the most promising woman in technology. She was the youngest self-made female billionaire in history. She was beautiful, charismatic, and was sure to change the world. She believed herself—and others predicted her—to be the next Steve Jobs. Her signature black turtlenecks were just one more way to emulate him. She was the female hero the tech world had been craving. Unfortunately, it was all a lie.

Bad Blood is the true story of one of the darlings of Silicon Valley and her dramatic fall from grace, written by the *Wall Street Journal* reporter who first broke the story in 2016.

KEY TAKEAWAYS & ANALYSIS

Key Takeaway: From a very young age, Elizabeth Holmes was driven to succeed.

Elizabeth came from a family of successful entrepreneurs. At the age of ten she wanted to be "a billionaire" when she grew up. She was driven and relentless. She was accepted to Stanford to study chemical engineering with an eye for biotechnology in the spring of 2002. Just a year later, she dropped out to start her own company.

Key Takeaway: Holmes was more concerned with money than with making a viable product.

Relying on wealthy friends of the family, the nineteen-year-old college dropout raised more than $6 million dollars for an impossible product. She pitched a diagnostic patch that would draw blood through "micro-needles" while simultaneously analyzing the blood in order to more effectively deliver medications and provide information to doctors. As this product was simply something she dreamed up—not something based in accessible technology—the idea was eventually pared down to just the blood sample diagnosis.

Key Takeaway: Elizabeth's concept for the "Theranos 1.0" had no basis in available technology.

Her adjusted vision was of a portable blood analysis system that was so small it could fit in the palm of your hand. She wanted it to function on a single drop of blood while providing detailed analysis that usually required a human to manually perform with a much larger blood sample. She believed it would save millions of lives of people who were overprescribed drugs with adverse side effects, who were constantly getting blood taken to have their dosages adjusted. The problem was that the prototype didn't work. There wasn't enough blood. The "box" was too small. The samples were contaminated as they moved through the different stages of microfluidic analysis. Elizabeth's personal fear of needles meant she refused to allow any more than a drop of blood to be used.

Key Takeaway: Holmes would fire anyone who didn't believe in the future of Theranos.

Chief engineer Ed Ku just couldn't get around the issues with the microfluid contamination. There were too many steps in too small a space, and the results weren't reliable. The device wasn't ready for the in-home trials that Holmes had prematurely agreed to with Pfizer. These were real people's lives at stake, people with terminal diseases, and Ku was concerned they had jumped the gun.

In response to Ku's inability to deliver, Elizabeth Holmes hired a competing engineering team within her own company. This team moved away from the concept of microfluidics and instead aimed to robotize the human process of pipetting samples and mixing them with reagents, all within the portable box. Though bigger than the toaster-sized Theranos 1.0, the Edison—or the "glue bot," as it was derisively referred to—was already more reliable than the original. Unfortunately, it was still leagues away from a finished product. Shortly thereafter, Ed Ku and his entire team were fired.

Key Takeaway: The company culture at Theranos was clouded with suspicion and distrust.

Holmes didn't trust anyone and was constantly worried that company secrets were being divulged. She set up silos within the company and forbade contact between teams with each team reporting only to her. Beyond just decreasing morale, this severely affected the company's ability to get anything done. One day, she fired someone for plugging in a USB port to their desktop. In fact, people were constantly getting fired without explanation. Everyone was on edge and no one was allowed to speak to anyone else about it. Holmes's second-in-command, Sunny Balwani had everyone's emails meticulously searched for evidence of betrayal.

The rampant suspicion was to a point—Elizabeth demanded unflinching loyalty from her staff. If ever there was a hint of questioning, uncertainty, or outright dissent, that person was fired without a word or a second thought. Holmes would then have someone go through their emails in order to create a blackmail file that could be used against them. Rather than the exception, this was common practice.

Key Takeaway: Some board members began to question the company's promise.

Elizabeth continued to present overly rosy projections to the board based on supposed contracts with multiple pharmaceutical companies that never seemed to materialize. When asked to present these contracts, they were always "wrapped up in legal" or she "didn't have any copies on hand."

Avie Tevanian, a former Apple executive, a friend of Steve Jobs, and a board member who had invested $1.5 million noticed that in the course of a year, the entire executive team had turned over. He also noticed that the issues stopping the Edison (the successor to the Theranos 1.0) from launching were completely different than the previous year. How was that possible for a product that was supposedly almost ready to hit the market?

When Avie brought these concerns up to the chairman, he was asked to leave the board and sell his shares at a significant discount. When he objected, Elizabeth threatened to sue him. Avie, a multi-millionaire in his own right, walked away from the board and from his money without looking back.

Key Takeaway: Elizabeth got people to believe in a vision and to forget the faulty product.

Elizabeth continued to tout Edison as "the iPod of health care" despite its myriad issues. She arranged for trials with different companies, contracts all hinging on the reliability of the product, when the Edison couldn't even make it through a sales pitch without malfunctioning. Elizabeth never blinked. She assured investors it was not an issue and carried on. If the box didn't perform in the upcoming trials however, any projected revenue would be lost. That was the least of their problems.

Beyond the implications of a product that doesn't work or the defrauding of investors, there is a reason there is so much regulation in the healthcare space: lives are at risk. Holmes continuously plays this card in her speeches and public appearances, evoking the pain and trauma that terminal patients endure with endless blood samples and lengthy wait times for results. The Edison was supposed to fix that.

Doctors use blood tests to make innumerable decisions including adjusting dosages, changing medications entirely, and ordering often expensive tests and potentially dangerous procedures. If the samples from the devices aren't accurate, patients will suffer. Despite this reality, Holmes is unflappable as she pitches the technology as both reliable and revolutionary. People believed in her vision.

Key Takeaway: A family friend takes out a competing patent.

The childhood neighbor of the Holmeses, Richard Fuisz, was known for his vindictive nature. Fuisz was in the business of patents and inventions in the healthcare space. He was irked when he discovered that Elizabeth, the daughter of his wife's long-time friend and once neighbor, had entered the business without consulting him. His revenge was to patent a part of the Theranos system that he could later license back to her. He filed a patent for the mechanism by which doctors would be alerted to abnormal blood results in April 2006, which he estimated at around $4 million in value. Elizabeth didn't learn of it until January 2008, by which time the Fuiszes and Holmeses had already stopped speaking to one another. At this point, Fuisz was referring to his patent as "the Theranos Killer."

Though she tried to sue him for patent infringement, Fuisz's son worked at the law firm representing Theranos at the time, and so they declined to move forward with the case.

Key Takeaway: Elizabeth's second-in-command is a mysterious, suspicious, and unstable man.

Sunny Balwani, Elizabeth's long-time live-in boyfriend, is an Indian-American man twenty years her senior who purportedly made $40 million in a start-up just before the dot-com bubble burst. Yet there was almost nothing about him on the internet before this story broke. He also worked for Theranos, though his exact expertise was a point of mystery. His presence was dominating, threatening, and getting on his bad side meant getting "disappeared" from the company for good. Only sycophants and brownnosers had any chance of getting promoted. Despite he and Elizabeth living together, their relationship status was hidden from the board and other key investors. Everyone who worked there, however, seemed to be aware of it. Both he and Elizabeth maintained an air of defensive secrecy at all times.

Key Takeaway: The Edison continued to be plagued by glaring faults.

Elizabeth hired her best friend from college, Chelsea, to join the sales team with Sunny. As she and Sunny were out making pitches, they were confronted with issues. The Edison never seemed to work properly—the results were consistently inconsistent. Sunny blamed the issues on poor wireless connectivity (which was one of the issues to be sure), but Chelsea began to understand that the real problems ran far deeper. After befriending one of the engineers, she learned that there still wasn't enough blood to run the samples; they were overdiluted, which produced often tainted results. The machines couldn't run if it was too hot or too cold by even a few degrees. Patients themselves had trouble operating the machines, though they were touted as "in-home" devices. Pfizer had backed out of their deal after their trial produced underwhelming and undependable analysis.

When Sunny and Chelsea headed to Mexico with the Edisons during the peak of the swine flu outbreak, machines were once again riddled with errors. Eventually, Chelsea's issues with Sunny's lies, and her ethical qualms with the state of the Edison, led her to walk away from her long-time friend and from Theranos for good.

Key Takeaway: Theranos struck deals with Walgreens and Safeway despite a lack of results.

In 2010, Theranos struck up a $50 million deal with Walgreens to utilize their Edison boxes in drugstores across the country. Every Walgreens would contain an in-store lab promising blood results in under an hour on 192 different tests. No matter that the Edison wasn't capable of half of the tests on the list that required entirely different methods to perform; Elizabeth assured Walgreens the Edison could do it.

Top executives at Walgreens were enamored with Holmes and believed missing this opportunity would be the mistake of a lifetime. Their excitement, however, led to vast oversight. When Walgreens executives came to see the lab at Theranos they were denied access and offered weak excuses as to the refusal. Security was so tight they were followed to the bathroom during the meeting. No one at Walgreens ever saw the "Edison lab" at Theranos—because it didn't actually exist. Despite the president of Walgreens' pharmacy business getting his finger pricked by the Edison, he never received the test results. Elizabeth and Sunny refused when a man on the project at Walgreens wanted to do a comparative test on the results from the Edison against those from Stanford Hospital. Walgreens had no proof whatsoever that these devices worked, and somehow, no one at Walgreens seemed to be concerned by that.

At the same time, Elizabeth struck a similar deal with Safeway grocery stores. While neither Walgreens nor Safeway were happy with the lack of exclusivity in their deals, they were both relieved just to be a part of what they saw as an unmissable opportunity.

Key Takeaway: Chaos continued to reign at Theranos.

In order to deliver on their promises to Walgreens and Safeway, Theranos had to design a completely new box monikered, the miniLab. This new box would be capable of the multiple types of analysis required to perform all 192 blood tests that Walgreens required. Elizabeth and Sunny had promised this was not only possible, but already completed before the company even began working on it.

At the same time, nepotism at the company was rampant. Elizabeth hired her brother two years out of college with no relevant experience or training to run the product management team. He, in turn, hired a bunch of his frat brothers from Duke University to work under him. Despite none of them having experience in blood work or medical testing, they endeared themselves to Elizabeth and quickly moved to the top of the delicate hierarchy she and Sunny created.

The air at Theranos was tense with distrust. Sunny continued his rampage of firing employees for even the appearance of a slight against him or failing loyalty to the company. He surrounded himself with Indian engineers with little experience in the field who were willing to defer to his ultimate authority. He fired those who didn't do the same in a humiliating parade of having their belongings searched for company property and being marched out by security that became all too familiar to those who had been there for years. Many new hires in the company quit as soon as they began to understand how unhealthy Sunny and Elizabeth's management style truly was.

Key Takeaway: Safeway's CEO falls victim to Elizabeth's charms.

In 2012, as the Safeway project was, in theory, getting ready to roll out, Safeway CEO Steve Burd decided they would get started by having Theranos machines test blood at one of their employee health centers. The strange part was that the boxes weren't being used to test the blood; traditional methods involving phlebotomists and hypodermic needles were used instead. Instead of the results being instantaneous, some were taking up to two weeks to come back. And the loudest alarm bell was that employees were getting wildly inaccurate results—saying their samples indicated they had prostate cancer when they were perfectly healthy, for example. When these concerns were brought up to Burd, he quickly dismissed them. He was firmly under Elizabeth's spell—she could do no wrong.

Unbeknownst to Safeway, the tests were being performed in a poorly-run Theranos lab in Palo Alto while others were being outsourced to an independent lab, and not a single Theranos proprietary device was being used.

When another year had passed without a launch of the mysterious Safeway "wellness play," Steve Burd was asked to resign as CEO.

Key Takeaway: A military deal comes close to exposing Theranos's secret.

In attempting to strike a deal with the U.S. military to use Theranos boxes on the battlefield in Afghanistan, Elizabeth found a close ally in Four-Star General James "Mad Dog" Mattis. She also inadvertently exposed herself to FDA regulation.

Lieutenant Colonel Shoemaker, after hearing Theranos's pitch, raised his regulatory concerns both to Elizabeth and to contacts of his at the FDA. Elizabeth dismissed him offhand, but Shoemaker's emails led to a surprise inspection of the Theranos lab. Though there was nothing egregiously out of order with the lab operations (after all, they weren't even operating any Theranos devices), the inspection set Elizabeth off on the war path.

When General Mattis came to her defense, he and L
Shoemaker came up with an inventive solution that would
allow Theranos to start testing soldiers' blood without going
through the time-consuming FDA regulatory hurdles. The
results would be tested against previous samples taken to
determine accuracy and could start immediately.

Inexplicably, Theranos never got back to them about
beginning the trials.

Key Takeaway: Theranos sues Fuisz.

In 2011, Richard Fuisz was served with papers for patent
theft against Theranos for his bar code mechanism that
would alert doctors of changes in patients' blood. Elizabeth
Holmes alleged that Richard's son John had stolen
proprietary information leading to the patent while working
at the law firm that represented Theranos back in 2006, and
then gave that information to his father's company, Fuisz
Pharmaceuticals.

The bar code patent wasn't stolen; John Fuisz had never
discussed the technology or even accessed Theranos's files
while he worked at the firm. His father developed the patent
on his own and had a long email trail to prove it. He
developed it specifically to mess with Elizabeth, simply out
of vengeance.

That didn't stop Elizabeth from hiring one of the most
expensive attorneys in the country and paying him $4.5
million in Theranos stock to take the case. Boies, the most

igator in the country, now had a vested interest
s of Theranos.

Key Takeaway: The price of dissent increases.

"It's a folie à deux...the presence of the same or similar delusional ideas in two persons closely associated with one another." (Ian Gibbons, p. 144).

Ian Gibbons was the first experienced scientist hired at Theranos back in 2005. His name is on all of the original patents, along with Elizabeth's despite her having little to do with the science. His specialty is in immunoassays—the type of blood test that the Theranos 1.0 and the Edison relied upon. He was being called to testify in the patent case.

Ian worked tirelessly for Theranos, and for a long time was in the good graces of Elizabeth and Sunny. Until he wasn't. Ian was a stickler for detail and insisted that the tests inside the Edison perform as reliably as those in a lab. Of course, they never did. Over time, he was demoted, then fired, then rehired at an even lower position, until eventually he was completely ignored.

The job was too much stress; his ostracization depressed him. He was overwhelmed with anxiety. The cries for help were there, but no one heard them, not even his wife. On the day before his deposition in the patent case—when Theranos lawyers tried to convince him to use a doctor's note to avoid appearing—he committed suicide. After working at Theranos for ten years, almost no one at the company was informed, and no memorial service was held.

Key Takeaway: The runway to launch faces new obstacles.

Before Theranos was to make their launch public, they needed some fresh branding for the company. Naturally, Elizabeth's obsession with emulating Steve Jobs led her to Chiat/Day—the same company that handled many of Apple's iconic campaigns.

As usual, some at Chiat/Day were enamored with Elizabeth, while others were suspicious. Holmes insisted upon making wild, unsubstantiated claims on the website about the accuracy of Theranos's tests. As false advertising is illegal, and especially fraught in the healthcare space, some of the ad team members were hesitant. They asked to see verification of these claims, but never received it; they were extremely concerned for the legal liability of Chiat/Day.

On the night before the website was to launch, Theranos decided to scale back the language without warning. "A drop of blood is all it takes" was changed to "A few drops is all it takes." Claims about accuracy, the size of the sample needed, the time to receive results, the ability to do all tests through the finger prick rather than venously—all of these things were walked back at the last minute. People at Chiat/Day were growing increasingly wary.

Key Takeaway: As public launch approached, Theranos was nowhere near ready to go live.

As turnover continued, new faces were presented with the bleak reality of the miniLab: it was far from ready. Theranos needed a machine for Walgreens by February 1, 2013 in exchange for a $100 million "innovation investment" and a $40 million loan. That deadline had now come and gone. Holmes was determined to have a product by September, despite the technology being years away from patient-ready.

As the launch date grew ever closer, more employees resigned due to ethical concerns. How could you launch in Walgreens stores when the machines were so error prone? When the technology was so far from complete? Anyone who raised concerns of this nature was seen as a cynic, a naysayer, and an enemy of the project, and was promptly fired.

In Sunny's words, "anyone not prepared to show complete devotion and unmitigated loyalty to the company should 'get the fuck out'" (Carreyrou, p. 173).

Key Takeaway: Theranos' valuation continued to balloon.

Just before the official launch was set in September 2013, Holmes used the positive press from a *Wall Street Journal* editorial she finagled about herself and her "miracle technology" to do yet another capital raise. This time, she valued Theranos at $6 billion. Seven years before, the valuation was a meager $40 million.

Theranos wasn't alone: in the early 2010s private companies such as Uber and Spotify were fetching multi-billion-dollar valuations as well, raising hundreds of millions in capital of their own. The difference, of course, is that their technology actually worked.

Elizabeth and Sunny were claiming to have solved problems that had plagued an entire branch of bioengineering and microfluidics for decades. The different types of tests needed—from immunoassays and hematology assays— needed their own samples to be completed. The same tiny finger prick just couldn't do it. But the secretive power-couple presented another story to their latest round of investors: a story where their machines could perform 99 percent of tests performed in a lab, and one where the results were exactly as accurate. Their board of directors stacked with seasoned billionaires and men such as General Mattis only lent further to their credibility.

In 2014, venture capital group Partner Fund purchased $96 million of Theranos stock for $17 a share. That brought the current valuation up to $9 billion, and Elizabeth's personal net worth up to $5 billion.

Key Takeaway: Cherry-picking data became the rule in testing the Edison and miniLab.

Theranos continued to hire new members on all of its teams, many of whom came in excited only to be quickly deflated at the reality of operations. Tests were consistently failing. Data was being manipulated. No self-respecting scientist would allow these numbers to be presented as truth.

As samples began to come in from the now operational lab in the Palo Alto Walgreens, the Edison consistently failed routine quality control checks. Instead of taking the machine offline and recalibrating, a newly hired lab tech was instructed to take 12 different results, discard the outliers, and present the mean of those findings as the accurate analysis. This was far beyond any lab protocol she had ever witnessed.

The Theranos website continued to claim their tests had "a less than 10 percent coefficient of variation" (the limit set to determine the accuracy of a test) despite their CV often being many multiples higher. Despite these glaring inaccuracies, Theranos expanded into forty consumer Walgreens' locations in Arizona.

Key Takeaway: Theranos was cheating at state proficiency tests.

After discovering that Theranos was using machines built by other manufacturers, and not the Edison, to remain compliant with health codes, an employee brought this concern to Elizabeth and Sunny. He believed they were cheating on these proficiency tests, but he was assured that everything was above the board. When he went to confirm this claim with the testing authority, he learned that what they were doing was illegal. He then anonymously reported Theranos to the New York heath department.

That employee happened to be the grandson of George Shultz, one of the most prestigious members of the board, once secretary of state, and a close family friend of the Holmes's. Despite his grandson's pleas as to their wrongdoing, Shultz remained a steadfast supporter of Elizabeth's to the end, eventually becoming estranged from his own grandson in Elizabeth's favor. Tyler Shultz resigned shortly after he discovered the fraudulent testing.

Key Takeaway: Richard Fuisz decided to settle with Theranos.

After an embarrassing performance in which he was caught lying on the witness stand, and realizing he was outgunned legally, Richard Fuisz decided it was time to settle. He and Elizabeth's attorney, Boies, agreed that Fuisz would withdraw his patent in exchange for Elizabeth withdrawing her suit. No money would change hands. Elizabeth had won.

Key Takeaway: Elizabeth embraced her newfound fame.

After Holmes was featured on the cover of *Fortune* in June of 2014, her celebrity exploded. She was suddenly "the youngest female self-made billionaire." She was giving constant TV appearances and interviews; she doubled her security team and began flying solely in her private jet. All of her dreams of becoming the next Steve Jobs or Bill Gates were being realized, and she was more than happy to play the part of a woman who was truly saving the world.

Key Takeaway: Alan Beam, the new lab director, tries to take a stand against Theranos.

Alan's concerns grew quickly in his first few months at Theranos. He began emailing himself results against company policy as proof that he had discussed issues with Sunny and Elizabeth, and proof that they were disregarding them. He was sure they were gaming the proficiency tests that Tyler Shultz had tried to blow the whistle on before quitting. He wasn't even allowed to see the quality control data any longer—a huge red flag for a lab director. He reached out to a law firm that specialized in corporate whistleblowers, but they didn't follow up. When he couldn't handle it any longer, he quit. Sunny brought him in to sign an affidavit confirming he was not in possession of any emails or hardcopies of any documents from his time at Theranos. He refused. Sunny threatened a lawsuit and Beam prepared to lawyer up. But the Boies legal team was too strong; Alan couldn't fight them alone. His lawyer instructed him to delete all 175 emails he had saved and sign the affidavit.

Key Takeaway: A small group led by Fuisz began to dig deeper.

After the lawsuit, Fuisz wasn't ready to give up. He knew something was wrong. He was joined by Rochelle, (the wife of Ian Gibbons, the engineer who committed suicide) as well as a pathologist named Adam Clapper who saw a piece on Holmes in the *New Yorker* and was immediately skeptical about the technology. The team of three eventually found Alan Beam on LinkedIn. They now had someone once on the inside to confirm their suspicions.

Beam, though terrified, set up a call with Fuisz and told him everything that had been happening at Theranos: the wildly inaccurate results, the falsified regulatory testing, the use of third-party equipment to perform tests, management's insistence to proceed despite constant warnings—everything.

Key Takeaway: Adam Clapper took the story to the Wall Street Journal.

Clapper had a contact at WSJ—John Carreyrou. He was intrigued and set up a time to meet with a reluctant Alan Beam. Beam confirmed in person everything Clapper had alleged. The machines didn't work; the results were completely unreliable to the point of being ridiculous;

Theranos was breaking federal law with their proficiency testing. Clapper also found it interesting that Elizabeth had been hiding her relationship with Sunny from the board. If that was a secret, how many other secrets was she willing to keep from them?

Carreyrou began digging in and soon realized the story had merit. He chased after any previous Theranos employees, though most weren't willing to talk. Then Carreyrou managed to get in touch with Tyler Shultz: the grandson of the board member who chose Elizabeth over his own family. Tyler was more than willing to talk.

Key Takeaway: The emotional and financial costs of inaccurate results become clear.

In Carreyrou's investigation, he comes across a woman who received results from a Theranos test showing she had extremely high levels of calcium, protein, glucose, and three liver enzymes. Because of these results, along with a ringing in her ear that turned out to be due to lack of sleep, her doctor was worried she was at risk for a stroke. She underwent multiple tests including a CT scan and two MRIs. Every one of her tests at the hospital—including her blood tests—came back completely normal. But Maureen Glunz was forced to pay $3000 out-of-pocket for the additional testing due to the high premiums on her health insurance.

Glunz wasn't the only one forced to endure these unnecessary costs. The list of patients whose lives had been affected by their false-positive results continued to grow as Carreyrou continued to dig. Luckily, most of them had gotten a second opinion and discovered their results were normal before changing their dosage or switching medications entirely. But the implications of this deception were abundantly clear: lives were at stake.

Key Takeaway: Theranos goes after Tyler Shultz.

In the process of the investigation surrounding the *Wall Street Journal* article, Theranos discovers that Tyler Shultz is one of the informants. Despite Tyler's grandfather being on the board, the lawyers come after him hard, pressuring him to sign away his rights and snitch on any other former Theranos employees speaking to the press. Tyler refused and is assured Theranos will be suing him for breach of his confidentiality agreement. But for some reason, they decide to put the suit on hold. As negotiations continue, Tyler is pressured hard by Boies's firm to give in to their demands. They threaten to bankrupt his entire family with legal fees if he doesn't cooperate. Though Tyler never caves, he is forced into hiding after his family is separated and the threats begin to impact his daily life.

Key Takeaway: Theranos resorts to any means possible to squash the article.

After reaching out to Holmes multiple times for a meeting and being constantly denied, Carreyrou is fed up. The *Journal* won't publish a story of this nature without letting the subjects know exactly what they're going to say and allowing them to comment. Meanwhile, Holmes is busy making appearances on everything from Jim Cramer to Charlie Rose. She's avoiding Carreyrou, no question. When Carreyrou finally gets in a room with Theranos months later, Elizabeth isn't even there. David Young—the head of the biomath team and an unflinching loyalist to the Theranos fabrication—is joined by a team of powerful attorneys. This is not a friendly meeting.

The legal team argued that Carreyrou's questions about their practices amounted to asking for trade secrets. They refused to answer questions about how many tests were actually performed on the Edison versus the other commercial sampling machines that were known to be in their lab. They insisted those machines were for comparing results, not for patient analysis.

After the meeting is over, Boies's legal team starts threatening anyone who spoke to Carreyrou. Sources are being followed. They are being threatened with lawsuits. Sunny even threatened one of the doctors who spoke on the record about the inconsistent results she witnessed. Yet another doctor was told her "life would be ruined" if she spoke out against Theranos.

To top it all off, the *Wall Street Journal* was threatened with exposing trade secrets and defamation; the paper would be sued if they ran the piece.

"It dawned on me that there was nothing these people would stop at to make my story go away" (Carreyrou, p. 258).

Key Takeaway: Holmes was ready to launch the miniLab with improved falsified techniques.

In summer of 2015, Theranos was still going strong. With the release of the miniLab, they had fixed the Edison's glaring issue of producing an error message when a sample wasn't properly analyzed, which happened all the time. Instead, they designed an app that, when given an error message by the machine, slowed the completion meter considerably, stalling out at around 60 or 70 percent complete. When the people waiting on the tests would finally leave, they would then run the samples through the commercial analyzers they had purchased and send them the results later via email. This way an error message would never be seen, and a "slower" results was much easier to explain away.

In order to continue fleecing the FDA, Holmes voluntarily submitted certain tests—ones that had a *Yes* or *No* answer versus ones that were sensitive to levels in the blood. This way, she appeared to be gaining FDA approval.

Key Takeaway: Rupert Murdoch, who owned the parent company of the Wall Street Journal, was now the largest investor in Theranos.

Holmes seemed to have everyone under her thumb. Everyone believed she was the real deal, and her enigmatic presence drew people in. Murdoch asked around about Holmes and heard nothing but rich and powerful people singing her praises. Rupert Murdoch invested $125 million in Theranos in a round that raised $430 million. It was the biggest investment in a single company he had ever made.

It was clear Holmes was trying to use Murdoch's power over the *Wall Street Journal* to kill the article, visiting his offices and pleading multiple times after his investment, but Murdoch deferred. He assured her that the paper wouldn't publish anything if it were false.

Key Takeaway: On October 15, 2015 the story was published in the Wall Street Journal.

The reaction was mixed. Some in Silicon Valley came to her defense. Others finally had confirmed what they had long been suspicious of. Holmes, however, held her ground. She insisted the story was a complete lie and that their technology did everything it claimed to do. After the article's release, the FDA was prompted to do a surprise inspection of Theranos's labs. In doing so, they declared the nanotainer—the tiny container used to hold those tiny blood samples—an "uncleared medical device" and banned its use. It was an intentional play on their part. They effectively shut down Theranos with the decision.

Key Takeaway: Rather than concede defeat, Elizabeth Holmes dug in.

Holmes was set to appear at a three-day conference ironically hosted by the *Wall Street Journal*. The conference had been planned long before the article broke, and everyone agreed it was best not to change anything. Holmes, rather than apologize or equivocate, took the opportunity during her thirty-minute speech to double down on every lie she had ever told.

She insisted that they paused use of the nanotainers by choice. She claimed they had never used commercial machines to replace their finger-stick tests. She stood by their proficiency testing methods, even asserting they had the "express blessing of regulators." Most egregious of all, she made the claim that they had never diluted samples in order to run them through commercial analyzers—despite this being the entire crux of their operation.

Their unreliable results depended solely on the dilution of samples into commercial machines jerry-rigged for their smaller sample sizes.

Key Takeaway: Theranos loses federal certification.

Despite their ability to mislead federal regulators for years—hiding labs, misdirecting, and delaying—Theranos was finally subject to an investigation by the Centers for Medicare and Medicaid Services. When they found numerous deficiencies, CMS gave them time to rectify the issues, which Sunny blamed on "the end of the fiscal year and a new round of investors" taking up their time.

Theranos was keeping the report from being released under the guise of "trade secrets." When CMS finally released a letter detailing their findings, it was damning: Theranos posed "immediate jeopardy to patient health and safety."

The entire 121-page report confirmed the rest. The Edison machines were wildly unreliable, and most of Theranos's tests were performed on commercial analyzers.

In a follow-up, CMS accused Theranos of failing to correct 43 of 45 deficiencies found in their original report. In a desperate bid to avoid losing certification, Holmes voided hundreds of Edison's test results—essentially admitting the Edison didn't work at all.

On June 12th, 2016, Walgreens discovered the voided blood tests that Homles had tried to hide and dissolved their partnership. That July, CMS banned Theranos and Holmes from participating in the lab business for two years.

Key Takeaway: After regulatory failure, the lawsuits followed, and the money disappeared.

Holmes and Theranos were sued by their venture capital firm, by Walgreens, by other investors, and by patients alleging consumer fraud and medical battery. They were forced to shut down their labs in Palo Alto and in Phoenix and ordered to pay $4.65 million in reimbursements to the residents of Arizona.

Theranos spent most of the $900 million they had raised settling lawsuits and various debts, though Holmes attempted to hang on by a thread, even publishing a poorly-received paper on the miniLab. That is, until the Securities and Exchange Commission charged Theranos, Holmes, and now-ousted COO, Sunny Balwani with conducting an "elaborate, years-long fraud." It is presumable both Balwani and Holmes will be wrapped up in litigation for some time to come.

EDITORIAL REVIEW

John Carreyrou's true tale of an entrepreneurial hero fallen from grace is juicy, detailed, and near incredulous at times. As you turn each page you can hardly believe she got away with all of this for so long, raising almost a billion dollars in the process. How did this woman pull the wool over the eyes of so many for so long? How did she trick CEOs, billionaires, and four-star generals alike? Carreyrou would have you believe her lies ran on charisma and secrecy. She would stop at nothing to protect her secret, and her off-putting charm left people dazzled into believing.

The book is thoroughly researched and provides detailed accounts from various sources, relaying everything from meeting minutes, to heated exchanges with lawyers, and threats issued by Sunny and Elizabeth that they surely never thought would get out—hence their obsession with confidentiality agreements. With each new defector from the walls of Theranos, another piece of the puzzle falls into place. The tale is no less bizarre once the story starts to break and we see Holmes beginning to squirm as her secret may no longer be safe. The wild threats, private investigators, and having innocent people followed paint a picture of a crazed woman willing to do anything to stop the truth from coming out.

Carreyrou's writing is compelling and exciting and makes the complicated science behind the story easy to follow. Not once as a reader are you bogged down with overly-scientific explanations of the devices, but you understand the fraud behind their operation without issue. Presumably, this was one of the cruxes of Holmes's deceit: most people investing didn't comprehend the technology behind what she was claiming to do. Those who did were the ones who declined to invest.

Overall, the story is riveting in its unraveling and is worth a read by anyone—not just those interested in behind-the-scenes looks at Silicon Valley. Carreyrou is a seasoned and respected reporter, and this book, without a doubt, upholds his legacy.

BACKGROUND ON AUTHOR

John Carreyrou has been a member of the *Wall Street Journal*'s investigative reporting team since 1999. He is currently the bureau chief for health and sciences for the paper in New York. He received his bachelor's degree from Duke University and has received two Pulitzer Prizes for his work, one for a 2003 piece that exposed corporate scandals in America, and the other for a 2015 piece on the Medicare system. His reporting on the Theranos story garnered a George Polk Award in Journalism for Financial Reporting.

Bad Blood is his first full-length book and is being turned into a movie starring Jennifer Lawrence as Elizabeth Holmes.

Carreyrou currently lives in Brooklyn with his wife and three children.

END OF BOOK SUMMARY

*If you enjoyed this **ZIP Reads** publication,
we encourage you to purchase a copy of
the original book from.*

*We'd also love an honest review on
Amazon.com!*

Made in the USA
San Bernardino, CA
18 April 2019